CW00539778

# MUSHROOM MISCELLANY

ADELE NOZEDAR

William Collins
An imprint of HarperCollins*Publishers*
1 London Bridge Street
London SE1 9GF
WilliamCollinsBooks.com

HarperCollins*Publishers*
Macken House, 39/40 Mayor Street Upper,
Dublin 1, D01 C9W8, Ireland

First published by William Collins in 2024

1 3 5 7 9 10 8 6 4 2



Written by Adele Nozedar
Front cover illustrations by AnitaPol
Interior illustrations by AnitaPol and Lisa Alderson
Design by Jacqui Caulton and e-Digital Design
Picture research by Milena Harrison-Gray
Editorial Director: Caitlin Doyle



A catalogue record for this book is available from the British Library

ISBN 978-0-00-871442-0



Printed and bound in Bosnia and Herzegovina

**DISCLAIMER**

**The publishers urge readers to cautious in the handling and consumption of any wild mushrooms. Do not consume any mushroom, unless you are certain of its identification and safety. This book is not intended for use as an identification guide for consumption, and the publishers cannot be held liable for any consequences of ingesting mushrooms. Some individuals are allergic to even mushrooms classified as edible, so check medical advice. Additionally, please familiarize yourself with local foraging restrictions and safety measures.**

# MUSHROOM MISCELLANY

Featuring Fun Facts,
Mushroom Profiles,
Recipes & More

**ADELE NOZEDAR**

# CONTENTS

FASCINATED
BY FUNGI

For a long time people believed that absolutely every living thing on the planet belonged to just one of two categories, or "kingdoms:" Animalia (animals) and Plantae (plants). Eventually, as knowledge of microscopic organisms grew, these two kingdoms of life became four.

Then in the late 1960s, an American ecologist called Robert Whittaker proposed a new classification system for living things that comprised a total of five kingdoms. As The Beatles were exploring transcendental meditation, and the hippy fraternity in San Francisco grooved blissfully in the Summer of Love, Whittaker quietly turned the planet on its axis with his discovery that fungi were not plant organisms, as previously thought, but were in a group all of their own. Thus was the kingdom of fungi introduced!

Whittaker had made a momentous discovery. He had noticed something that no one else had before—that fungi of all kinds, shapes, and sizes were essential in helping various organisms to decompose.

## Say hello to the Wood Wide Web

Imagine if everything on the planet remained intact. For example, if car parts never got rusty. Or if leaves never rotted down. Or if the bodies of deceased humans or animals remained as they were—intact, but no longer alive. Grizzly thought, isn't it? Our world would be buried under bodies, fallen trees, and detritus piled high, leaving our soil infertile and therefore useless. In turn, this would mean that we had no food!

The complications, when you start to think about them, are frightening. Life on Earth, as we know it, would no longer exist.

So here's where we got lucky with what is sometimes called the Wood Wide Web—an underground web of plant and tree roots, bacteria, and fungi, or mycorrhizal networks. We now know that mycorrhizal networks existed long before mankind, having been around for some 450 million years. (We are comparative newcomers; modern humans only arrived at the party a mere 200,000 years ago.)

The word *mycorrhiza* comes from the Greek *mukès*, meaning "fungus," and *rhiza*, meaning "root." It refers to what is a symbiotic relationship between fungi and plant roots—one that's mutually beneficial to both.

*So what exactly is a mushroom?*

A mushroom is in fact only one part of the whole organism. It is the fruiting body of certain types of fungi—effectively, a spore-spreading machine. Most of a fungus exists on or under the soil in the form of a mycelium, which is a continuously growing network of branching filaments (hyphae) that dissolve and absorb nutrients from their environment. It's possible to observe these fine white threads for yourself, usually if you turn over a rotting tree. If you do uncover any, though, make sure you gently replace the tree so that the hyphae can continue doing their job.

Put simply, in a forest, fungi absorb the carbon-rich sugar that is produced by trees during photosynthesis via their roots. In exchange, trees acquire nutrients such as nitrogen and phosphorus from fungi, which are able to absorb them from the soil.

What's even more exciting is that the Wood Wide Web may facilitate an exchange of resources. In his book *The Hidden Life of Trees*, the renowned German forester Peter Wohlleben suggests that trees and fungi are able to "share information"—about an abundance or scarcity of water, for example, or an aphid attack. When you think about it, this ability to cooperate simply and effectively is quite inspirational. We humans are a clever species—incredibly creative and able to solve problems in innovative ways—but we also experience separation and disconnectedness.

Trees, on the other hand, are part of an entire connected system. Whether it's the great redwoods of California or the ancient oaks of Britain, their roots reach down and form a remarkable and complex network, interwoven with fungi and interconnected by them, with each organism able to serve its own needs as well as contribute to the needs of others. If ever there was a time for us to recognize the importance of trees, especially older trees, it is now.

Until recently, we were not really aware of the underground networks that sustain our forests. One of the books that changed this was Canadian forestry ecologist Suzanne Simard's *Finding the Mother Tree*, which was published in 2021 and swiftly became a bestseller. (It was actually Simard who coined the phrase Wood Wide Web, back in the 1990s, drawing on the parallels with the interconnected nature of the World Wide Web.) Before training as a scientist, Simard had grown up in the Canadian forests—her extended family worked in the logging industry—and she gradually came to learn from her own first-hand experience and close observations that trees were much more important than she had previously realized. Her fundamental realization was that some trees connect with one another to share resources. However, not all trees—or fungi—act in the same way.

# Different types of fungi

There are three main kinds of fungi.

The most common type is **saprophytic fungi**. As the name indicates, these get their nutrition from dead organic matter, such as plants, animal bones, and feces. Although this may seem repugnant, saprophytic fungi are incredibly beneficial. These include a wide range of mushrooms and fungus—among these are jelly ear, morels, and truffles.

Next up are **parasitic fungi**, which absorb nutrients from a living host, including living plant matter. These often weaken, damage, or even kill their host. Two examples of diseases caused by parasitic fungi are "chestnut blight," which has decimated chestnut trees in the US, and Dutch elm disease. European elms have suffered so much from the latter that they are no longer seen as often as they once were. Honey fungus is also extremely destructive, and you'll learn more about this notorious example later in this book.

The third type is **mycorrhizal (symbiotic) fungi**. As we've already seen, this forms an underground network, a go-between that connects the roots of trees or plants. These fungi help plants access essential nutrients from the soil, and in return the

plants provide the fungi with the sugars that they are unable to produce themselves. To underscore the importance of these networks, the total length of fungal mycelium in the top 4 inches (10 cm) of soil is equivalent to half the width of our galaxy, which certainly gives pause for thought! Who knew that something so tiny could be so vital to life on this planet?

Having established a brief overview of the fungi kingdom, it's time to zero in on that specific part of a fungus called a mushroom. This is the part of the fungus that sprouts above ground—a fleshy, umbrella-shaped body, responsible for producing the spores that allow the fungus to reproduce. If you're curious to learn all about just some of the vast array of different mushrooms out there, read on!

In most climates, mushrooms grow all year round—and everywhere! Not purely relegated to woodlands and fields, mushrooms and fungi can be found in gardens, parks, walkways, and sometimes even where you would least expect them. However, fall/autumn is the height of the season, making it the best time to actually spot mushrooms during their ideal growing conditions. Immediately after rain—and for up to two to three weeks after a downpour—is the best time to spot mushrooms during any season, as the dampness triggers the fruiting process, sometimes even overnight. If you want to learn more about how and when to forage for mushrooms, sign up for a mushroom-foraging tour in your local area.

All of a sudden, it seems, mushrooms are everywhere. How, or why, has this happened?

Mushrooms have been topping food trend lists and rising steadily in food store sales and foraging tours. In 2022, *The New York Times* even named the mushroom as "Ingredient of the Year." Renowned experts in the field of mycology suddenly found that their books were piled high in bookshops. Netflix gave us the beautiful *Fantastic Fungi* documentary. Renowned writer and journalist Michael Pollan astonished us with *How To Change Your Mind*, all about the "new" realm of psychedelics, purporting ideas about dying, addiction, and transcendence, unlikely to have been a mainstream mega hit even a few short years ago.

The burgeoning trend for eating less meat has an important part to play in the upsurge of interest, too. Mushrooms—which we now know are closer to us than plants—have come into their own. Rich, umami meat substitutes, a planet-friendly source of vitamins, minerals, protein, and fiber, can now be found readily in supermarkets, whereas just a little while ago only specialist whole-food stores sold such items.

Added to this, foraging for fungi and other wild foods means that those of us who know what's what end up showing others how to find them, use them, and eat them, making new careers where previously this was the province of the serial nerd. What accelerated this passion, though?

Then there was lockdown. Remember that? It seems a lifetime ago. Perhaps it gave some of us time to think about the bigger picture. Foraging for wild food, including fungi, was becoming popular prior to 2020, and it is possible that the search for all things natural was accelerated by the pandemic, since many of us suddenly had time on our hands to look carefully at our immediate locale.

Our love for mushrooms is really about our love for the entire planet, and this book is a celebration of that. In it, we seek to pull together all the strands that bind us, just like mycelium, to areas of enquiry, questions not yet answered, and ideas not yet born. In the illustrated pages that follow, you'll be astonished by the incredible range of species out there, and all they have to offer—from mushrooms as medicines and cooking ingredients, to mushrooms as specimens of fantastic beauty and wonder. This book serves as a love letter to mushrooms, helping readers discover more about these incredible beauties connecting our world; it can also be used as an identification guide, recipe prompt, and imparter of fabulously fun facts. Welcome to *Mushroom Miscellany*.

# Parts of a mushroom

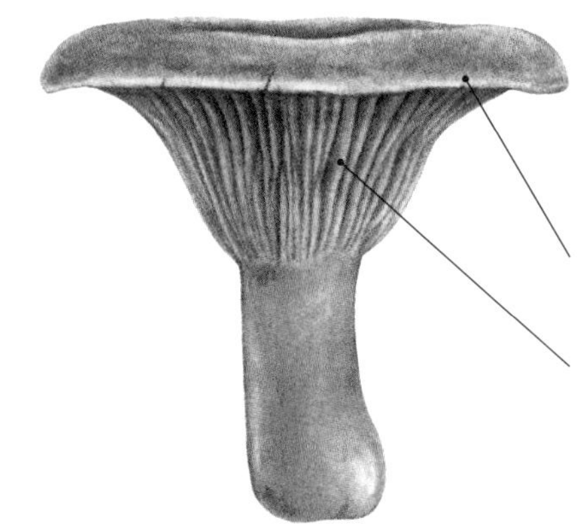

Saffron Milkcap

Rim, or edge

Gills (found on the underside of the cap). These can be attached to the stem, run down the stem, or only under the cap.

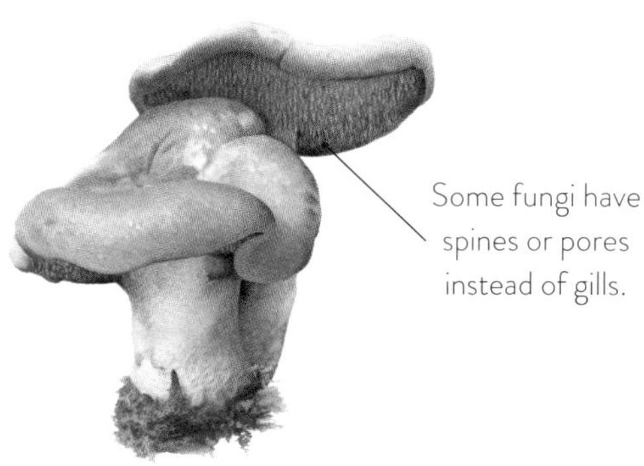

Some fungi have spines or pores instead of gills.

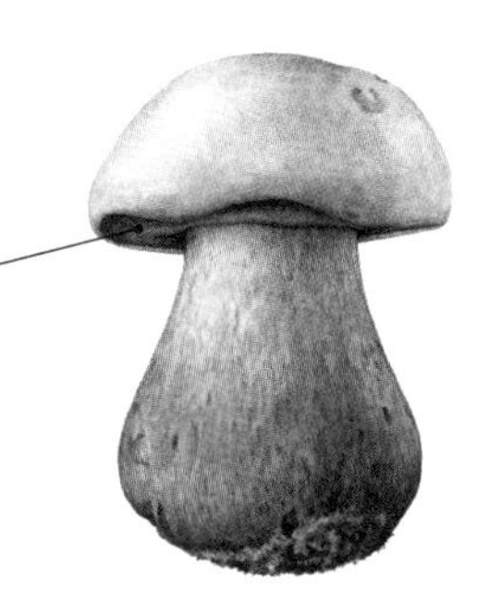

Hedgehog Mushroom

Satan's Bolete

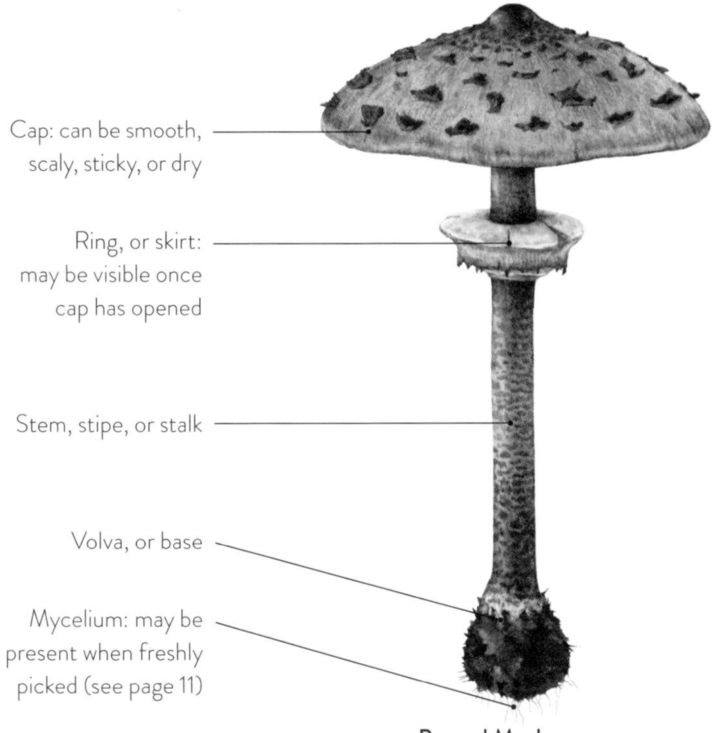


Parasol Mushroom

Non-standard forms include bracket, cup, and jelly fungi.

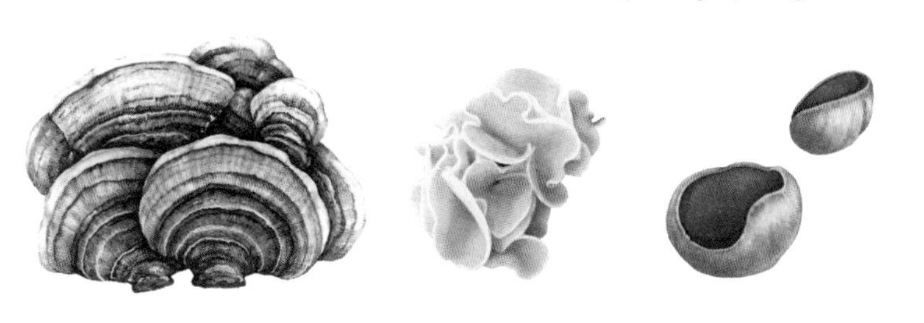

Turkey Tail Mushroom | Witches' Butter | Scarlet Elf Caps/Cups

DISCLAIMER

The following profiles include both edible and inedible mushrooms. It's worth knowing that some mushrooms appear to be harmless when, in fact, they are toxic. Additionally, some can have dangerous doppelgangers, so always exercise caution. If you're not certain about a particular specimen, do not handle or consume it. Never pick any fungus that you cannot identify with absolute certainty. Where a mushroom's conservation status has been assessed by the IUCN, this is included in its entry.

Be aware, too, that some individuals may have an allergic reaction to what's considered a "safe" fungus for most people.

# MUSHROOM PROFILES

# Shaggy Ink Cap or Lawyer's Wig

*Coprinus comatus*

**FOUND:** Temporal and boreal regions of Europe and North America; widely introduced elsewhere

**TYPE:** Edible

Often seen growing on lawns and in graveled areas, this fungus can appear in the same place in successive years. It grows to between 2 and 6 inches (5–15 cm) high, usually in clusters. A young Ink Cap is smooth to the touch. As it ages, the cap reveals its scales, or telltale "lawyer's wig"—hence its common name; *comatus* is Latin for "long-haired." The gills turn from creamy white to pink and finally black, dissolving into dark fluid in a process called "deliquescence." When harvesting, beware of slugs that may be hiding in the uppermost part of the mushroom.

The black liquid produced by the Shaggy Ink Cap was used as an ink substitute in the 17th and 18th centuries. Recently, it was used for the wonderful illustrations in Merlin Sheldrake's book *Entangled Life*. To try using it yourself, find six mushrooms, leave them to turn black, then strain the "juice." Add a drop of thyme oil to mask the smell, then apply the ink with a brush or pen nib. Avoid using a good-quality fountain pen because the ink will ruin it.

Young Shaggy Ink Caps (at their all-white stage) are tasty. The flavor is best when eaten within six hours of harvesting. The Shaggy Ink Cap is listed as of "Least Concern" according to IUCN's Red List of conservation.

# Hedgehog Mushroom or Pig's Trotter

*Hydnum repandum*

**FOUND:** Temperate and boreal regions of Europe and North America; widely introduced elsewhere

**TYPE:** Edible

The cap of this pale cream-colored mushroom grows to between 1 and 7 inches (around 3–17 cm) in diameter, and it has a distinct velvety texture. Its downy stem, or stipe, often sits off-center. The mushroom has a pleasant fragrance and it gets its name from the creamy pink "spines" found on the underside of the cap and partway down its stem, which grow to a few millimeters in length. They are not sharp by any means, but are nevertheless reminiscent of a hedgehog's spines. Fungi belonging to the genus *Hydnum* are notable for having these spines, or teeth, instead of gills. *Hydnum* comes from the Greek *hudnon*, meaning "truffle," while *repandum* means "turned up," relating to the mushroom's shape. Alternative names include Sweet Tooth and Sheep's Foot Mushroom.

The Hedgehog Mushroom is found hiding in mossy grass underneath pine, spruce, and birch trees in the later part of the year, and it's often easy to pick the entire fungus. Its relative *Hydnum rufescens* (the Terracotta Hedgehog) is named for its darker reddish color. Both mushrooms are renowned for their delicious flavor and texture. The Hedgehog Mushroom is listed as of "Least Concern" according to IUCN's Red List of conservation.

# Field or Meadow Mushroom

*Agaricus campestris*

**FOUND:** Worldwide

**TYPE:** Edible

This mushroom is possibly one of the most well known of all, and easy to find, with the habitat matching the name (in Latin, *campestris* means "of the field"). Wide open spaces, such as pastureland or sports fields, are ideal places to search, but these mushrooms can also be found on the edge of woodlands, and in gardens. The cap grows quickly, up to 4 inches (10 cm) or more in diameter, flattening out as it does so, and if you're lucky you might see hundreds of these 'shrooms that have popped up first thing in the morning where, just a few hours ago, there was nothing to see!

The cap of a perfect young mushroom is creamy white on the top, with pinkish gills beneath that turn brown as the mushroom matures. It also has a satisfyingly fragrant scent. After washing, these fungi can be eaten raw. The firm stem is also edible. The Meadow Mushroom is listed as of "Least Concern" according to IUCN's Red List of conservation.

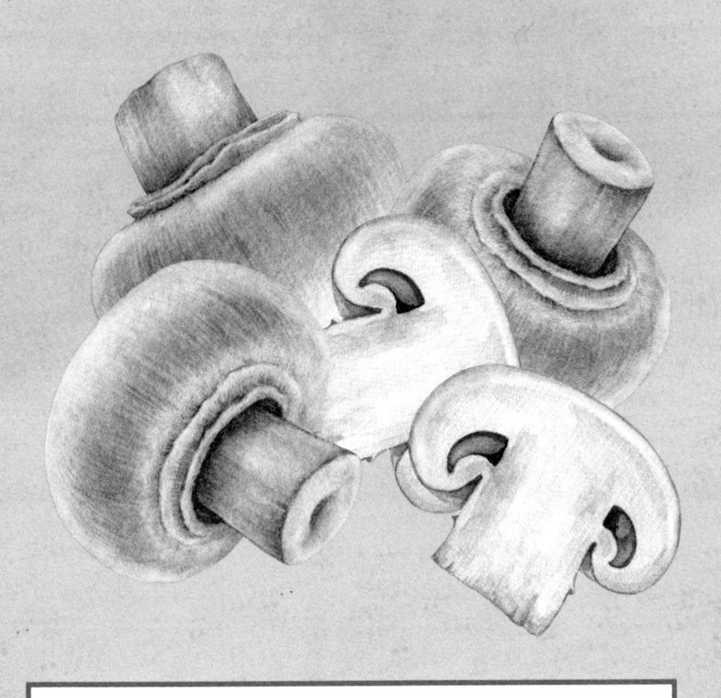

**☠ DANGEROUS LOOKALIKE ALERT ☠**

Two of the "Destroying Angel" group of fungi—*Amanita virosa* and *Amanita hygroscopica*—can look very similar to the Meadow Mushroom, and both are deadly poisonous (see page 34). The distinguishing feature is a volva at the base, absent in the Meadow Mushroom. Less dangerous, but still able to cause a stomach upset, is the Yellow Stainer (*Agaricus xanthodermus*). For identification, this one stains yellow if cut or bruised.

# Button Mushroom or Portobello

*Agaricus bisporus*

**FOUND:** Worldwide

**TYPE:** Edible

This mushroom has a wide variety of names, according to its age and color. For example, the immature white mushroom might be referred to as a common or table mushroom, or a champignon, while older specimens with browner caps are known as Italian brown, cremini, chestnut, or portobello mushrooms.

Although common and therefore relatively easy to find in the wild, most people use storebought button mushrooms of both colors; they're cheap, widely available, and, unlike mushrooms picked in the field, they're as clean as a whistle, so they're appetizing to eat raw as well as cooked. For this we have Louis Lambert to thank—an American mycologist who found a specimen on his farm in Pennsylvania back in the 1920s and began to cultivate it. The little fungus, literally as neat as a button, quickly found favor. It's amazing to think that that one small white mushroom went on to generate so many millions more!

# Chanterelle or Girolle

*Cantharellus cibarius*

**FOUND:** North and Central America, Europe, Eurasia, and Africa

**TYPE:** Edible

The Chanterelle is possibly one of the most delicious of all edible mushrooms, prized for its flavor as well as its golden color and apricot-like aroma. Although Chanterelles tend to be associated with French cuisine, they are also very popular throughout the rest of Europe and in the United States, where they are found in deciduous or coniferous forests. A lucky forager will spot these gold-colored disks from a distance, scattered over the forest floor, just waiting to be gathered and eaten.

The funnel-shaped cap of the Chanterelle measures some 4 inches (10 cm) across, with wavy edges and a depressed center, and veins on the underside running down to the stem. The mushroom's name was inspired by its shape, deriving from *kantharos*, a type of drinking vessel used in ancient Greece that featured a pedestal and a cup that widened toward the top. The German name for these beauties is Pfifferling, which refers to their peppery flavor.

# Death Cap or Deadly Amanita

*Amanita phalloides*

**FOUND:** Temperate and boreal regions of Europe; introduced to many other parts of the world

**TYPE:** ☠ Poisonous ☠

With a name like this there can be no confusion—this mushroom is deadly. Identifying the Death Cap can be tricky because it's similar in appearance to other edible species, such as Caesar's Mushroom (*Amanita caesarea*). The Death Cap is an imposing specimen, with a domed cap that grows up to 6 inches (15 cm) across, and reaching the same in height. The cap is usually white, pale green, or yellow; the stem is mainly white but may have a greenish tinge. The Death Cap has a faintly sweet smell that becomes more potent and sickly as the mushroom matures.

*Amanita phalloides* is generally the culprit whenever a mushroom-related death is reported. If ingested, symptoms such as fever and vomiting may occur after around eight hours, followed by a latent phase. However, the toxins remain active in the body and, if treatment is not sought, signs of liver and kidney damage will appear some days later, which will prove fatal without extreme intervention in the form of a liver transplant. Interestingly, the Death Cap is believed to be the fungus that killed the Roman emperor Claudius, having been served to him by his wife Agrippina, added to a dish of harmless Caesar's Mushrooms.

# Destroying Angel

*Amanita* species

**FOUND:** Temperate and boreal regions of Europe and North America

**TYPE:** ☠ Poisonous ☠

Four different species of mushroom share this forbidding name. In Europe there are *Amanita virosa* (European Destroying Angel) and *Amanita verna* (Fool's Mushroom, or Spring Destroying Angel), while in North America there are *Amanita bisporigera* and *Amanita ocreata* (found in the west and east respectively).

All four share the following characteristics: a white stalk and gills, and, most notably, a membrane that encapsulates the young mushroom like an egg, then breaks as it grows, remaining as a cuplike form (a "volva") at the base of the mature mushroom. The mature cap measures from 2 to 5 inches (5–12 cm) across, on a stem ranging from 3½ to 6 inches (9–15 cm) tall. Destroying Angels are found in mixed deciduous woodland, as well as in more urban areas.

It's always worth being very wary of any fungi that you're not absolutely certain about. Destroying Angels can fool even seasoned experts because it's easy to mistake them for common Meadow Mushrooms (see page 26). A Destroying Angel has white gills, whereas a Meadow Mushroom's gills are pink or brown. Young Destroying Angels can also look very similar to Puffballs. To be sure, cut your specimen in half—a Puffball will be smooth and white throughout, whereas the inside of a young Destroying Angel will reveal gills or a stem starting to form.

# Giant Puffball

*Calvatia gigantea*

**FOUND:** Temperate regions worldwide

**TYPE:** Edible

A pristine, creamy white Giant Puffball is a happy sight for a forager. Often found growing in long grass, they can be mistaken for a soccer ball, although they're sometimes smaller—and sometimes larger! The mushroom has no stem, and its body can reach up to 20 inches (50 cm) in both height and width. Giant Puffballs are easy to dislodge from their hold in the ground and they can appear all year round, but are most commonly found in early spring or fall.

Giant Puffballs are only edible when young, when their flesh is white, fresh, and spongey. Once their color has started to change, spores are present and they can cause digestive issues. After harvesting, their flesh will quickly become discolored and start to smell, so they must be used straight away. The taste is good, with a texture that mimics meat (see page 130 for a simple recipe). Interestingly, the Giant Puffball also has a history of use in folk medicine—traditionally used, for example, by some Indigenous American cultures to dress wounds.

# Deadly Webcap

*Cortinarius rubellus*

**FOUND:** Northern regions in the U.K., Europe, and North America

**TYPE:** ☠ ☠ Highly poisonous ☠ ☠

Usually found in coniferous forests, *Cortinarius rubellus* is one of seven species of fungus belonging to a group called Orellani, all of which contain the mycotoxin orellane. Nicholas Evans, author of the best-selling novel *The Horse Whisperer*, was famously poisoned by a Deadly Webcap while on vacation with family in Scotland back in 2008. Having gathered what they believed to be ceps (Penny Buns; see page 53), they cooked the mushrooms and ate them, but quickly fell ill, eventually needing to have kidney transplants. The lesson here is clear. This mushroom is to be admired only—avoid touching it, and never consume it.

The mushroom's common name refers to the weblike structure ("cortina") that protects the immature gills. It also goes by the name of Fool's Webcap. The cap itself, grubby orange in color, is initially convex, flattening as it matures, often with a central hump, or umbo, on the top. The diameter of the fully open cap reaches 1½ to 3 inches (4–8 cm). The stem is sometimes bowed, and paler than the cap.

# Turkey Tail

*Trametes versicolor*

**FOUND:** Worldwide

**TYPE:** Edible

This is a very beautiful fungus; *versicolor* refers to the bands of different colors on top of the cap. Named for its resemblance to a wild turkey's tail feathers, it also belongs to the group of fungi known as "bracket fungi," or "shelf fungi," which grow on logs and trees in shelf-like formations. A Turkey Tail can reach 4 inches (10 cm) in diameter, and up to 3 mm thick, overlapping to form clusters.

Although not actually toxic, the woody toughness of the Turkey Tail renders it inedible. It has no discernible smell or flavor. It's thought to have health benefits, however, tackling bacteria, fungi, and viruses, so it is widely available for sale in capsule form—and it may even be beneficial as a supplement for those undergoing cancer treatment. As more scientific research is carried out, it will be exciting to see just what this mushroom has to offer. And in the meantime, we can always appreciate the Turkey Tail for its beauty.

# Beefsteak Fungus

*Fistulina hepatica*

**FOUND:** U.K., Europe, North America, North and South Africa, and Australia

**TYPE:** Edible

The cap of this bracket fungus (see page 41) grows to as large as 12 inches (30 cm) across, and up to around 2 inches (5 cm) thick. It's shaped like a tongue, with an upper surface that's moist and shiny when young, becoming tacky and then tough as it matures.

Also known as the Poor Man's Steak, Beefsteak Polypore, or Ox Tongue, this unusual specimen looks just as its common names suggest. The "ripe" Beefsteak closely mimics the look and texture of a piece of raw meat, and the fact that its flesh oozes a bloodlike sap only enhances the resemblance—it's a sight that's disconcerting for meateaters and vegetarians alike!

If you'd like to find your own samples, keep your eyes peeled during the fall months and look out for rotting wood on sweet chestnuts or oaks in particular. You might spot Beefsteaks tucked inside the trees too, or halfway up, annoyingly out of reach.

Despite its appearance, the Beefsteak Fungus is suitable for eating raw as well as cooked. It has a piquant, slightly sour flavor that works well in salads. As with all fungi, though, make sure your mushrooms are clean and clear of insects and soil.

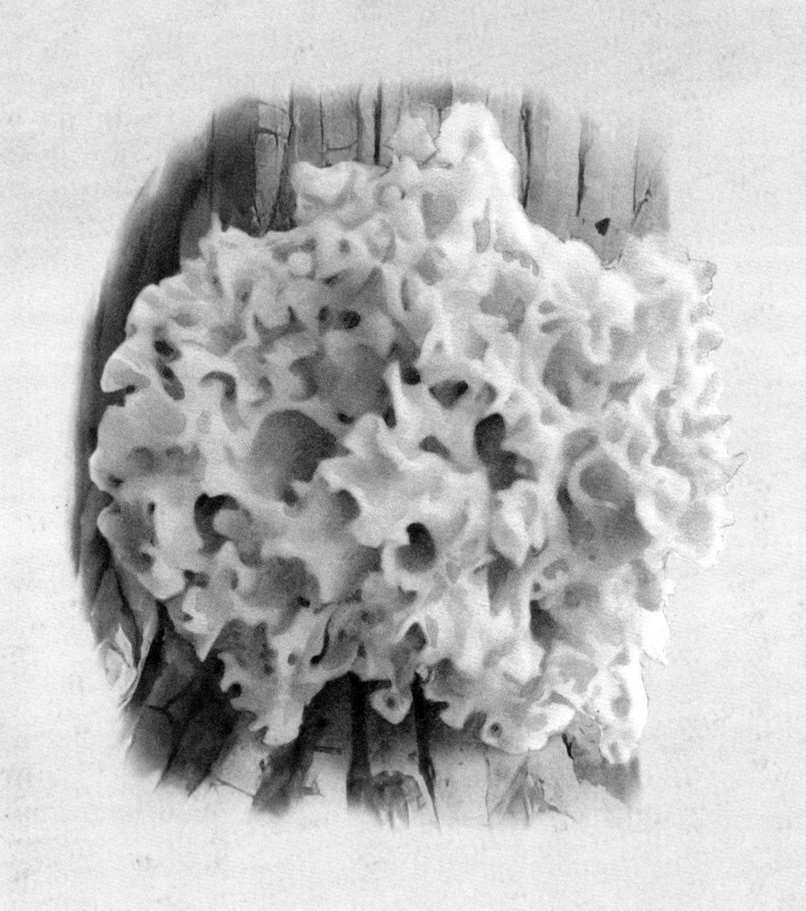

# Cauliflower Fungus

*Sparassis crispa*

**FOUND:** U.K., central and northern Europe, Asia, and North America

**TYPE:** Edible

The Cauliflower Fungus can grow to up to 10 inches (25 cm) tall, and up to 15 inches (40 cm) across. It is found growing at the base of conifers, particularly pine trees. *Sparassis* comes from the Greek verb "to tear," while *crispa* means "curly"—a reference to this mushroom's distinctive mass of curly fronds. Other common names include Wood Cauliflower and Brain Fungus, which are both apt titles for this lucky find.

Something of a chef's delicacy, the Cauliflower Fungus has an interesting and unexpected nutty flavor, with a slightly chewy texture. The downside is that, with all those folds, it's tricky to clean, but it's definitely worth the effort. (See page 126 for a recipe.)

Fungi have been used as traditional cures for centuries, and in recent years their use for medicinal purposes has increased around the world. *Sparassis* is no exception. It is said to have antifungal and antibiotic properties, with a range of different benefits. As with all the fungi in this book, scientific research confirming these healing properties is ongoing, but in the meantime, if you like the idea of trying this fungus but are unable to find it in the wild, it is now cultivated in Asia, North America, and elsewhere.

# Lion's Mane Mushroom

*Hericium erinaceus*

**FOUND:** Europe, North America, and Asia

**TYPE:** Edible

As you would expect for such a spectacular specimen, the Lion's Mane has many alternative names, including Bearded Hedgehog, Bearded Tooth Fungus, Monkey Head Mushroom, Tree Hedgehog, and Pom Pom Mushroom—all inspired by its dangling "spines."

Anyone attempting to find the Lion's Mane should look for badly diseased oak and beech trees. If you succeed, however, be sure to leave any specimens where they are. Although currently listed as "Least Concern" on the IUCN Red List, the Lion's Mane is said to be declining, and in the U.K., for example, it is illegal to pick them. A better way to sample this mushroom would be to buy a grow kit—these are now readily available and relatively cheap. The flavor of the Lion's Mane mimics that of seafood such as crab, scallops, or lobster.

Long used in traditional Chinese medicine, Lion's Mane is becoming increasingly popular as a supplement, potentially supporting the immune system, brain function, and gut health. It's available in liquid and powdered form, and the mushrooms can be eaten raw or cooked, but as always, err on the side of caution and only purchase from reputable suppliers.

# Brown Roll-rim or Common Roll-rim

*Paxillus involutus*

**FOUND:** Widespread in the northern hemisphere; introduced to Australia, New Zealand, South America, and South Africa

**TYPE:** ☠ Poisonous ☠

To the untrained eye—and sometimes even the trained one—this commonly occurring mushroom can look very much like many other brown mushrooms seen in mixed woodland and meadows. Its funnel-shaped cap grows to around 4¾ inches (12 cm) in diameter, with a slight dip in its center. It is a tawny color when young, deepening to a darker, sometimes blotchy, shade as it matures. The rim that gives this mushroom its name rolls under gently, with a sticky-looking wavy edge. When picked, the Roll-rim bruises a dark brown.

Interestingly, Roll-rims are still seen for sale in some countries, despite their toxicity. These mushrooms were actually once considered edible and although it may be possible to consume them without any issues, the consequences on other occasions can be extremely serious, and sometimes fatal, with deaths occurring annually.

# Waxcaps

*Hygrocybe*

**FOUND:** Worldwide, but particularly northern Europe and North America

**TYPE:** Edible

Waxcaps, or Waxy Caps (as they're called in some parts of the United States), are a group of mushrooms with caps that have a waxy sheen, becoming sticky or slimy when wet. They come in a variety of different colors—bright yellow, crimson, purple, pink—and some are nothing short of spectacular. Particularly lovely is the Parrot Waxcap, which ranges from green to yellow to blue, with a glistening cap and stem.

There are around 150 different *Hygrocybe* species found around the world (in Greek, *hygrocybe* means "watery head"). Although they grow in a range of different habitats (wooded areas, heathland, and even sand dunes) they prefer grassland areas that are poor in nutrients—called "waxcap grassland"—and they're also often found growing in graveyards, lawns, or pastures and meadows that have been neglected. Waxcap grasslands are now in decline in the U.K. and Europe due to agricultural practices, so these mushrooms are becoming increasingly scarce. A number of *Hygrocybe* species are now on the IUCN Red List, having been assessed as "Vulnerable" or "Endangered," so although some Waxcaps are edible, they're better left where they are.

# Penny Bun or Porcini

*Boletus edulis*

**FOUND:** Throughout the northern hemisphere: Europe, Asia, and North America

**TYPE:** Edible

The botanical name for this mushroom comes from the Latin *boletus*, meaning "mushroom," and *edulis* meaning "edible," which is very apt. Also referred to as a cep or a porcini, the Penny Bun is, as the name suggests, a generously rounded brown mushroom that's greatly sought after for its flavor. The fruiting body grows to between 3 and 12 inches (7–30 cm) and the paler-colored thick stem is edible too. It grows in both deciduous and coniferous forests, and if you want to go gathering, the season extends from midsummer to late fall.

As edible species go, this is one of the best, and well worth looking out for. There is also the unrelated Bay Bolete (*Imleria badia*), which is not quite as highly prized as *Boletus edulis*, but is a very worthwhile substitute—found in the same habitats in the fall months. The Penny Bun is listed as of "Least Concern" according to IUCN's Red List of conservation.

# Fly Agaric or Fly Amanita

*Amanita muscaria*

**FOUND:** Temperate and boreal regions of the northern hemisphere; introduced to much of the southern hemisphere

**TYPE:** ☠ Poisonous, hallucinogenic ☠

The Fly Agaric is arguably the most iconic mushroom of all, with its telltale red cap, white spots (warts), white gills, and tall white stem. It is so widely recognized that it has even appeared in numerous works of fiction. *Alice in Wonderland* features a hookah-smoking caterpillar who sits on the mushroom and lures Alice into taking a bite (hinting at its hallucinogenic properties), and Fly Agarics feature in the comic world of the *Smurfs* as well as the video-game franchise *Mario*.

Fly Agaric can be found in woodland, heathland, and even in gardens, and it prefers to grow beneath pine, spruce, and birch trees. It's quite a large mushroom when mature, with a cap that ranges from 4 to 8 inches (10–20 cm), and a stem that may reach as much as 9 inches (23 cm) in height. Some subspecies can have white or yellow caps in place of red.

Although toxic, these mushrooms have been used for shamanic or religious rituals in different cultures (see, for example, page 105). However, as with all "magic" mushrooms, effects can be very unpredictable, sometimes causing seizures or comas as well as a neurological disorder known as Alice in Wonderland syndrome, which distorts perception.

# Satan's Bolete or Devil's Bolete

*Rubroboletus satanas*

**FOUND:** Mostly U.K. and Europe

**TYPE:** ☠ Poisonous ☠

Previously known as *Boletus satanoides*, this is a member of the Boletaceae (bolete family). Despite being related to another bolete, the delicious Penny Bun (see page 53), the name of this mushroom (as well as its appearance) is like a warning: "DO NOT EAT ME!"

A rare mushroom, but useful to be able to identify, Satan's Bolete has a unique appearance. It is short and round, with a cap that can grow up to a mighty 20 inches (50 cm) in diameter; the cap is a grubby white, and the bulging stem below it is red. The flesh, when bruised or cut, turns blue, and it has an unpleasant odor.

Satan's Bolete prefers chalky soil and appears in the summer months and early fall. It is more commonly seen in the warmer regions of southern Europe, and has been sighted farther east, although climate change could well lead to changes in distribution in future.

Consuming this mushroom will usually lead to abdominal pain, vomiting, and diarrhea, particularly when eaten raw. Luckily, its bright coloring, imposing size, and smell make it easy to identify and avoid. The best advice if you come across *Boletus satanoides* is—admire it, but don't put it in the pot.

# Scarlet Elf Cup or Elf Cap

*Sarcoscypha austriaca* and *Sarcoscypha coccinea*

**FOUND:** Widespread, including Africa, Asia, Europe, North and South America, and Australia

**TYPE:** Edible

Many mushroom names are purely descriptive—and these two are prime examples. The name of the genus comes from the Greek *sarco*, meaning "flesh," and *skyphos*, meaning "drinking bowl," because the fruiting body of *Sarcoscypha* species takes the form of a "cup"—one that's smooth, irregularly shaped, and bright red (although the shade can vary), with a diameter ranging from ¾ to 2¾ inches (2–7 cm). The underside of the cup is paler, with a matte surface. The two species are easily mistaken for each other. The Scarlet Elf Cup is covered in tiny coiled hairs, whereas the hairs on the Ruby Elf Cup are not coiled—a difference that can only be seen through a microscope.

Elf Cups grow on twigs or dead branches, hidden away in the undergrowth or tucked away among damp mosses, unseen to all but the most observant eye. They appear in the late winter months, disappearing as soon as the weather gets warmer.

There are around 28 different *Sarcoscypha* species, including the two highlighted here. Both are considered edible, and their striking appearance makes them popular with innovative chefs. There is disagreement about whether they can be consumed raw, so it's best to play it safe (see page 134 for a recipe).

# Morel

## *Morchella esculenta*

**FOUND:** Northern hemisphere in particular, including North America, China, India, and Pakistan

**TYPE:** Edible

It's a very lucky day for anyone who finds this mushroom. Morels are arguably one of the most prized and delicious mushrooms of all, but finding them in the wild is akin to a treasure quest *à la Raiders of the Lost Ark*. It's worth knowing that there tend to be "hot spots"—places where Morels pop up at the same time every year, and it's reported that some such secret troves have been utilized and passed down for generations. The scent of a Morel is fragrant and earthy, and the taste, meaty and nutty.

A first step is to look for the trees that they favor—including ash, elm, and apple trees—but they can be found in a range of different habitats. You'll find identification very easy, though, if you do happen to find one; with its conical honeycomb structure, a Morel looks very much like a brain on a stick! The brown cap measures 1 to 3 inches (3–8 cm) across, and around 2 to 5 inches (5–12 cm) in height, and it sits atop a pale stem.

Do be aware that these mushrooms must be cooked before eating (see page 132 for a recipe), as they are toxic when raw. And because they are notoriously hard to find in the wild, you might want to try your hand with one of the many mushroom-growing kits available instead.

# Wood Ear or Jelly Ear

*Auricularia auricula-judae*

**FOUND:** Europe

**TYPE:** Edible

A Wood Ear is a bracket fungus (see page 41) with a very distinctive appearance. Brown, gelatinous, and fleshy, it looks very much like a human ear—*auricula* being the Latin for "ear." Its Latin name translates as "ear of Judas," deriving from its association with Judas, who according to myth hanged himself from an elder tree after betraying Jesus Christ. (The Wood Ear is often found growing in clusters on old or fallen elder-tree branches.)

An easy mushroom for beginners to identify, Wood Ear can be found throughout the year. It grows up to around 3½ inches (9 cm) across. Although edible, some people find it very bland, while others can be put off by its unsettling appearance! There are a few different *Auricularia* species found in other parts of the world, too—notably in Asia, where *Auricularia heimuer* (Black Ear Fungus) and *Auricularia cornea* (Cloud Ear Fungus) are very popular in cooking, due to their chewy texture and ability to soak up the flavors in a dish. Wood Ear is also thought to have health benefits, supposedly lowering cholesterol and enhancing gut health.

# Fool's Conecap

*Conocybe filaris*

**FOUND:** Europe, North America, and Asia

**TYPE:** ☠ ☠ Deadly poisonous ☠ ☠

This innocuous-looking specimen has a slender stem that can grow to around 2 inches (5 cm) in height, with a prominent ring. It's topped with a shiny orange-brown cap that's initially conical but flattens as it matures, with a small hump ("umbo") at its center. There are more than 200 *Conocybe* species, generally all with the same slim stem and pointed bell-shaped hat—often known as Dunce Caps or Coneheads for this reason. They can be found in lawns and in grassland, as well as in dead wood or grass, sand dunes, and even dung.

The word "fool" is generally an indication that a fungus is toxic, and this one is no exception. In common with the Death Cap (see page 33), *Conocybe filaris* contains alpha-amanitin, which damages the liver when ingested. Other conecap species contain the hallucinogens psilocybin and psilocin and these "magic mushrooms" have long been used for their mind-bending properties, despite their potential negative side effects.

Because the Fool's Conecap occurs so commonly and is so insignificant in appearance, it can be easy to mistake it for something more innocent—a salutary reminder to maintain a healthy respect for and distance from any fungus that you're not completely sure of.

# Orange Peel Fungus

*Aleuria aurantia*

**FOUND:** North America, Europe, and South America

**TYPE:** Edible

The Latin *arantia* means "orange," hence the name of this brightly colored fungus, which at first sight really does look like a discarded piece of orange peel. The "cup" typically grows up to 4 inches (10 cm) across—the size, in fact, of a small orange—and has wavy edges, forming a loose rosette shape that flattens with age, although it will often become misshapen if it's growing in a spot overcrowded with other mushrooms. As with carrots, its vivid color is caused by the presence of carotenoids, which are antioxidants—some people therefore believe the fungus may offer some of the same health benefits.

Orange Peel Fungus can generally be found in long grass or at the edges of paths or tracks. It likes poor soils that have been disturbed. In temperate regions it appears from September to January, and although widespread, it's not particularly common, but does tend to appear in the same patch year after year. Its taste, though, doesn't quite live up to expectations for some, being slightly tough and very mild in flavor. However, strips of its "peel" can brighten up a salad or cocktail.

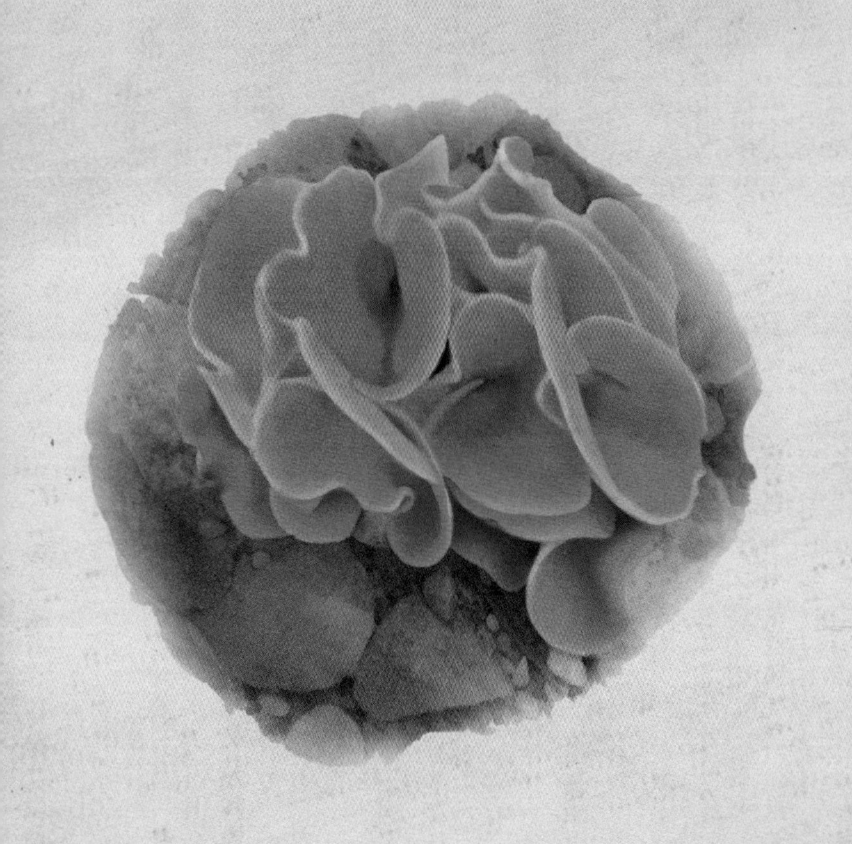

# The Sickener

*Russula emetica*

**FOUND:** Damp woodlands in the northern hemisphere

**TYPE:** ☠ Toxic ☠

The *Russula* genus comprises some 750 different species of mushroom, all of them relatively common and easy to find due to their bright colors, although the abundance of species—often scattered in and around mixed woodland—can make a definitive identification tricky. Also called "brittle gills," the stem is usually brittle enough that it will snap and give a clean break, rather than bend like the stems of other mushrooms.

As you can guess from its name, The Sickener is one of the more toxic varieties of this abundant group. It is bright red, fading in wet weather, and pink if cut. The cap is convex, with a smooth surface, measuring up to 4 inches (10 cm) across. The stem is white, sometimes yellowing as it ages. This mushroom has a fruity smell, and is said to taste peppery. Although boiling or pickling is believed to get rid of most of its toxins, it is nevertheless regarded as inedible. If eaten raw or perhaps as part of an ill-conceived fungi medley, a hapless diner will experience vomiting and diarrhea within hours. Elderly people or small children are most likely to suffer the worst effects, occasionally fatally.

# Oyster Mushroom

*Pleurotus ostreatus*

**FOUND:** Temperate and subtropical forests worldwide

**TYPE:** Edible

Named for its oyster-shaped cap, this is not only one of the tastiest mushrooms but also one of the most attractive. Its scent is clean and pleasant, and when cooked it has a nutty flavour that works especially well in Asian cuisine. The broad cap can be gray, white, or tan, and it generally measures from 2 to 10 inches (5–25 cm) across. The short, thick stem is often off-center. Oyster Mushrooms grow on hardwood trees, particularly beeches.

In addition to its flavor and beauty, the Oyster has an important ecological role to play via an interesting process called "mycoremediation"—essentially the use of fungi to remove human waste from the environment. Fungi produce enzymes that are able to break down pollutants in the soil, and *Pleurotus ostreatus* has been found to be a particularly effective mycoremediator, able to remove contaminants from both water and soil, often within a matter of days!

# Chicken of the Woods or Sulfur/Sulphur Shelf

*Laetiporus sulphureus*

**FOUND:** Europe and North America

**TYPE:** Edible*

Easy to find and identify, and delicious to eat, this has everything you could want in a mushroom. It is a bracket fungus (see page 41) and younger specimens are wavy-edged, soft, and spongy, becoming thinner and tougher with age until they eventually fade away until the following year. Individual brackets are thick and range from 2 to 10 inches (5–25 cm), and they grow in overlapping layers. Chicken of the Woods can be found from midsummer until fall, its bright burst of yellow often visible from quite a way off, once the forager learns to recognize it. This color deepens to orange as the fungi matures. Look for oak and chestnut trees, as well as their stumps, to find the mushroom.

**Take care to avoid Chicken of the Woods found growing on yew trees, which are poisonous and make the mushroom inedible.*

As edible wild fungi goes, Chicken of the Woods is one of the very best. As the name suggests, it resembles the color and texture of chicken. For vegans or vegetarians missing the umami kick of meat, this can be a very satisfying substitute—a recipe is provided on page 128.

**It's worth noting, though, that consuming it can cause stomach upset in some people, so sample it in small amounts to begin with, and do not eat it raw.*

# Hen of the Woods or Maitake

*Grifola frondosa*

**FOUND:** Europe, North America, China, and Japan

**TYPE:** Edible

Despite the similarity in name to Chicken of the Woods (page 73), Hen of the Woods is a different species altogether. While they share aspects of their appearance, with clusters of "feathers" overlapping one another, *Grifola frondosa* looks more like a brown lettuce—or hen! Its "shelves" grow in a circular formation, clustered to create a rather lovely rosette, some to 7 to 20 inches (20–50 cm) across. It is mostly found growing at the base of trees (in particular, old oaks) and is a perennial; that is, it appears regularly in the same place, year after year, in the fall months. If you find a patch, be sure to keep it a secret! As with Chicken of the Woods, this mushroom becomes darker as it matures and it will eventually rot away.

Hen of the Woods is also known as Maitake ("dancing mushroom"), and the King of Mushrooms in Japan, where it's particularly popular for both its earthy, nutty flavor and its reputed health benefits. Eaten while still fresh and flavorsome, it has a pleasant aroma that is strong enough that foragers may even smell it before spotting it. Maitake mushrooms are also sold in powdered form as a supplement.

# Liberty Cap

## *Psilocybe semilanceata*

**FOUND:** Temperate areas in the northern hemisphere, and occasionally the southern hemisphere

**TYPE:** ☠ Toxic, hallucinogenic ☠

*Psilocybe semilanceata* takes its common name from its cap's resemblance to the Phrygian cap—a tall, soft cap with a bent tip at the apex, worn in ancient times in Persepolis, in Iran, and elsewhere in the region. Later, the Roman goddess of freedom, Libertas, came to be depicted wearing the same style of cap (a *pileus*, as had been worn by the emancipated slaves of ancient Rome), which led in turn to the cap as a symbol of freedom during the American Revolution and, later, the French Revolution.

Liberty Caps are typically found in fields and grassland, and sometimes lawns and parks, and generally in wetter areas, in the later part of the year. The distinctive pointy cap sits on a spindly stem that grows to between 2 and 5 inches (5 and 14 cm) in height, making this mushroom difficult to mistake for any other.

This mushroom contains psilocybin and psilocin, so it has been used for recreational use as a hallucinogen. Consuming it may result in anxiety and paranoia, as well as physical symptoms including nausea, vomiting, and muscle weakness. The Liberty Cap is not the only hallucinogenic fungus, but it's certainly one of the best known.

# Parasol or Shaggy Parasol Mushroom

*Macrolepiota procera* and *Chlorophyllum rhacodes*

**FOUND:** Temperate regions of Eurasia (*Macrolepiota procera*), North America, Europe, southern Africa (*Chlorophyllum rhacodes*)

**TYPE:** Edible

The slightly larger Parasol Mushroom has a cap that appears as a pale brown sphere with a darker central "crown." The cap then expands into its flatter, fully opened "parasol." The stem can grow to 20 inches (50 cm)—bearing a double-edged ring that may remain or fall away—with the cap measuring the same in diameter. The Parasol Mushroom is occasionally called the Snake's Hat or Snake's Sponge, referring to the scaly pattern covering its surface. It can generally be found in grassy areas, growing near trees.

The Shaggy Parasol Mushroom is smaller, with height and cap width reaching around 8 inches (20 cm). Another notable difference between the two is that the Shaggy Parasol stem is a smooth off-white, whereas the Parasol Mushroom has "snakeskin" patterning. The Shaggy Parasol is found in mixed, shady woodland areas. Both mushrooms are nutty and earthy in flavor, prized by foragers and chefs alike. The umami flavor gets richer with age, and the mushrooms provide generous supplies, sometimes appearing in season up to four times a year. Although the tough stem is not eaten, it can be used to flavor stocks and sauces. The Shaggy Parasol is more likely to cause stomach upset if not cooked thoroughly.

# Amethyst Deceiver

## *Laccaria amethystina*

**FOUND:** Temperate regions in Europe, Asia, and North and South America

**TYPE:** Edible

This velvety purple fungus is strikingly pretty and, surprisingly, it's also edible. It's often found in hiding in the leaf litter of both deciduous and coniferous forests (near beech trees in particular) and even on grass verges. It reaches an average height of 4 inches (10 cm) and has a cap diameter of around 2 inches (5 cm). At first, the cap is convex, but it flattens as it matures, developing a depression at the center. Both the cap and stem are the same purple/lilac color, which fades with age, becoming a buff-colored memory of its former glory. This can sometimes make it difficult to identify, hence the name of "deceiver."

The Amethyst Deceiver is edible (although not particularly prized), but it has two lookalikes that share a similar habitat and contain toxic chemicals. These are the Lilac Fibercap (*Inocybe geophylla var. lilacina*) and the slightly larger Lilac Bonnet or Lilac Bellcap (*Mycena pura*). Ingesting either of these fungi can result in a range of physical symptoms, including sweating, vomiting, and blurred vision. Given that there are so many other delicious mushrooms, it makes sense to avoid the risk and leave the Amethyst Deceiver alone.

# Saffron Milkcap

*Lactarius deliciosus*

**FOUND:** Native to Europe; introduced to Australia

**TYPE:** Edible

Named for its distinct red–orange cap, this mushroom shares a symbiotic relationship with pine trees and is found exclusively in pine plantations and forests. This is why it's also commonly referred to as the Red Pine Mushroom. The stem is short and hollow, growing to about 1 to 2 inches (2–5 cm) high. The trumpet-shaped cap can grow to around 8 inches (20 cm) in diameter.

Although given the name *deliciosus* ("delicious") by Carl Linnaeus, who described it in 1753, it's thought that Linnaeus may have mistaken it for a different and more flavorsome Milkcap. The Saffron Milkcap can be bitter, but it's still a popular ingredient in the cuisines of several countries. In Poland, for example, they're served  in butter and cream. Russians preserve them in salt. And in Spain they're traditionally cooked with parsley, garlic, and olive oil. One thing to be aware of if you ever get to try this mushroom—if you eat enough of it, your urine will turn red. But since Saffron Milkcaps are known to be a source of vitamins and antioxidants, you might consider that a worthwhile side-effect!

# Honey Fungus or Bootlace Fungus

*Armillaria mellea*

**FOUND:** Worldwide

**TYPE:** Edible

Honey fungus is the common name for a number of different species of the *Armillaria* fungus, derived from their appearance—their caps are usually yellow or brown in color, and sticky when moist. Honey fungus is usually found growing in clumps on wood. Despite the innocuous name, this parasitic fungus can do irreparable damage to plants and trees. The alternative name of Bootlace Fungus comes from its long black rhizomorphs, which are rootlike structures that grow rapidly, below the surface of the soil, enabling the fungus to spread from one plant host to another. Rhizomorphs can travel long distances, hidden underground, with little to stop them.

*Armillaria mellea* has a stem that grows to 8 inches (20 cm) in height, with a ring near the top, and the cap is convex to begin with, becoming flatter as it matures. Although edible, some people are intolerant to Honey Fungus, so it's always best to consume this mushroom in small quantities to begin with.

Another interesting fact is that the largest living fungi on the planet happens to be a cousin of *Armillaria mellea*—an *Armillaria ostoyae*, thought to be thousands of years old (see page 90).

FUNGI
FUN FACTS

# What is a mushroom?

As we've seen, a mushroom is the fruiting body of a fungus, usually seen above ground. It releases the spores that produce successive generations of the fungus.

This description, however, is the very tip of a colossal iceberg. Scientists have been studying these incredible organisms for years and as soon as we think we have a grasp of the subject, more information is unearthed. We don't know, for example, exactly how many different species of fungus exist. So far, around 140,000 have been classified and named, but the total number is currently estimated to be as high as 3.8 million. Think about that for a moment. It's truly mind-blowing!

# What is a toadstool?

Generally, the term "mushroom" is used to refer to edible fungi, whereas "toadstool" is used for fungi that are poisonous. The tricky thing, though, is knowing which is which. In the story of *Alice in Wonderland*, the hookah-smoking Caterpillar enjoys a pipe of something that appears to be hallucinogenic—possibly the reason for the dreamlike state in which Alice finds herself . . . and let's not forget the Cheshire Cat!

# What's the largest organism in the world?

Yes, you guessed right, it's a fungus. What's more, one of the cousins of this prodigious organism is a very common one—a honey fungus found in domestic gardens the world over (see page 85). The big boy, though, is a gigantic *Armillaria ostoyae*, which resides in Oregon's Blue Mountains. Discovered in 1998, this fungus covers around 2,384 acres (965 hectares). It's believed to be at least 2,400 years old, and it may possibly have been around as long as 8,650 years, which would make it not only the biggest organism on the planet but one of the oldest too.

# Red Cage Fungus

Also called the Basket Stinkhorn, Latticed Stinkhorn, or, if you prefer, *Clathrus ruber* (*clathrus* is Greek for "cage" and *ruber* is Latin for "red"), this is a very odd-looking specimen indeed. Its unusual structure and coloring (the result of natural pigments) is a reminder of just how much variety there is in the wonderful world of mushrooms. Once found in the U.K. and central and southern Europe, the species has now spread to the rest of the world. It grows on decaying woody plant matter.

The Red Cage belongs to the Phallaceae family—known as the Stinkhorns. These are known for having a repugnant smell, similar to rotting meat. This might not be palatable for humans, but it is the perfect way of attracting flies and other insects, which unwittingly help to disperse its spores. It's not known with any certainty whether this fungus is edible, but the fetid stench of this rather beautiful specimen is enough for us to want to leave it alone.

# Building bricks from fungus



Do you like LEGO? Who doesn't! However, it's likely that you won't be aware of the role that fungus plays in the building blocks found in almost every child's toy collection.

Back in 1836, a Swiss pharmacist called Samuel Baup was the first to discover a particular byproduct in a distillate of citric acid. This byproduct became known as itaconic acid. Then, in the 1920s, itaconic acid was isolated from a fungus belonging to the *Aspergillus* genus. Before long, it began to be used in a wide range of industrial processes and to make paint, synthetic fibers, UV coatings, printing ink, resins . . . and LEGO!

# Tasty toasty tempeh

If you decide to eat toast for breakfast, but then discover your bread has gone moldy, you have a fungus to thank. *Rhizopus stolonifer*, also known by the common name of "black bread mold," is one of the first molds that will appear on bread, but you'll also spot it on other foods; it's one of the culprits behind what's called "soft rot" in strawberries.

If you've ever eaten tempeh, then you might be interested to know that it owes its existence to *Rhizopus oligosporus* or *Rhizopus oryzae*. Tempeh is made from fermented soybeans that are then packed into block form, and the fermentation process uses these fungi as a starter. Tempeh has minimal flavor, but it's good at soaking up added flavors, such as soy sauce.

Speaking of which, you'll probably be able to guess what that is made from. The fungi used to ferment the soybeans on this occasion are *Aspergillus sojae* or *Aspergillus oryzae*. *Aspergillus oryzae* also gives us two condiments commonly used in Japanese cuisine—miso, which is made from fermented soybeans, and mirin, which is a wine made from fermented soybeans or rice.

# Fungi for medicinal purposes

Hepatitis B is a liver infection caused by the hepatitis B virus and transmitted through blood. The vaccine that protects against it is made by using a very common household staple—baker's yeast, or brewer's yeast (*Saccharomyces cerevisiae*)—and small quantities of yeast proteins are present in the finished product.

Many common medicines are produced using fungi, and some of them employ antibiotics, which fight bacterial infections. One of the best known antibiotics is penicillin, discovered by the Scottish physician Alexander Fleming in 1928, when he returned home from a vacation to discover a mold—*Penicillium rubens*—growing in a petri dish of *Staphylococcus aureus*. Fleming noticed that the fungus seemed to be preventing the growth of the bacteria. He soon found that the mold produced a chemical that was able to kill bacteria, and he named this active agent penicillin. Scientists were later able to figure out how to extract purefied penicillin from the mold, and the rest is history.

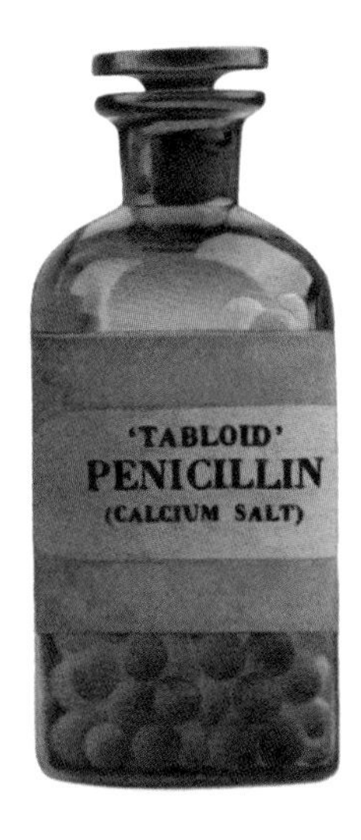

# The healing "caterpillar fungus"

Found in the Tibetan Plateau, *Cordyceps sinensis* (caterpillar fungus) has been used in traditional Chinese medicine for centuries. Like *Ophiocordyceps unilateralis* (see page 104), this is a fungus that lives on an insect host—in this case, the ghost moth. Spores of the fungus grow inside caterpillars, sending out hyphae that take over its entire body, and eventually producing a fruiting body that grows out of the dead caterpillar's head. The entire fungus–larva symbiote is collected for medical use, as well as re-created as a supplement in a lab. It's purported to have numerous medical and physical uses in traditional Chinese healing and, increasingly, Western medicine, including boosting immunity and invigorating the kidneys, treating impotence and fatigue, treating respiratory ailments such as asthma, and boosting exercise performance. Scientific studies are still being carried out to support this.

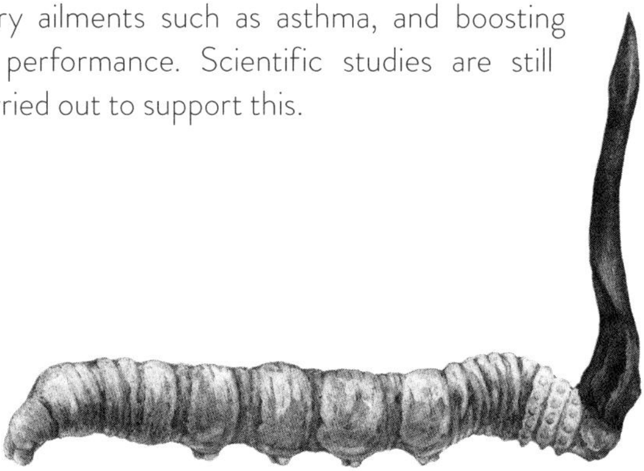

# Putting a foot in it

If you're suffering from athlete's foot, guess what caused it? Yes, a fungus! This infection can be caused by a number of different fungi, and it's not at all uncommon.

You might be interested (or perhaps alarmed) to learn that your feet may be home to as many as 100 different species. But when you consider that fungi thrive in warm, moist conditions, then it's easy to see how they survive on feet that are encased all day in warm socks and boots, or sweaty, tight-fitting sneakers, then are allowed to wander barefoot through the steamy changing rooms at a local pool, before being wrapped up for the night in cozy slippers. To a fungus, every one of these environments must seem like a party!

# Cheese feast

Did you know that without fungi, we would have a world without cheese?

The thought might be a bit offputting, but it's possible that cheese was discovered accidentally via the practice of storing milk in vessels made from animals' stomach linings. A key ingredient was (and still is) rennet, produced in the stomach. Rennet is used to coagulate milk and separate the solid curds from the liquid whey.

What has this to do with mushrooms, you might ask? Quite a lot. Microbes inadvertently came to the party, so to speak, bringing flavors and textures made as if by thin air ... which in fact is the case. Bacteria, yeasts, and molds are all found in cheese, and they are what give each cheese its distinctive taste. Some of the main fungi found on cheese include *Penicillium*, *Aspergillus*, and *Trichoderma*, and for some well-known cheeses, molds are deliberately added—*Penicillium*, for example, is used to make blue cheeses such as Roquefort, with their telltale "veins" of blue-green mold.

# Chocolate's secret ingredient

Believe it or not, without fungus, chocolate as we know it would not exist! That's because after ripe cacao pods have been harvested from the cacao tree, they are cracked open to access the beans and pulp within, then left to ferment in huge bins, waiting for the next part of the process. And that process is in fact the waiting itself. Where is the magic, you might ask—is it the beans themselves, or the pulp, which is rich in sugars?

The magic ingredient is actually in the air; fungal spores that ferment the sugars, triggering a series of chemical reactions that give the initially bitter and inedible beans the rich flavor that we appreciate so much. The fermentation process is responsible for other products too, with bacteria or yeast added to food sources to make increasingly popular health-giving foods such as sourdough bread, kefir, kombucha, yogurt, and cheese.

# Chaga

The botanical name of this curious fungus is *Inonotus obliquus*. A parasite that lives on the trunks of trees (mostly birch), it's found in the boreal forests of Canada, Alaska, Scandinavia, Russia, and China. The name chaga evolved from the Komi word for "mushroom," and the dark woody lump seen clinging to the tree is known as the "conk" (a sterile mycelium mass that gets its color from the presence of melatonin). It's also known as the Clinker Polypore, Birch Canker Polypore, and Cinder Conk.

Often referred to as a "super-fungi," chaga is thought to be a cure for various ailments, although more research is needed to gain a fuller understanding of its properties. In the meantime, although tricky to find in the wild, chaga is readily available to purchase online and from healthfood stores, and it's becoming popular as a hot beverage, made by brewing it in the form of a ground powder.

# Mushrooms that glow in the dark

There are at least 80 species of bioluminescent fungi found around the world. In India, some species of glowing fungi are called "electric mushrooms"—they live on bamboo and are so bright that the bamboo sticks are used by locals as natural torches! But why exactly do some fungi glow?

A group of researchers from the United States and Brazil thought that it might be a way for fungi to attract insects, which are responsible for helping distribute the spores that allow fungi to reproduce. One bioluminescent fungus, *Neonothopanus gardneri*, is found at the base of coconut palms in Brazil. Being protected by the trees, away from the wind, the distribution of spores becomes more difficult, so the researchers wondered whether bioluminescence provided a way to attract insects. They grew the fungi in a lab and discovered that the mushrooms glowed in a regular cycle, following a circadian rhythm, with their glow peaking at night—when spores are more active due to humidity. Further tests then showed that beetles were indeed drawn to this glow, indicating that the bioluminescence might have a role to play in reproduction.

# Natural-born killer of the fungal world

*Ophiocordyceps unilateralis* is commonly known as "zombie-ant fungus," and it's definitely one of the strangest organisms in this book. Its ghoulish ability to carry out "mind control" on an insect host has inspired storylines in several works of fiction, including the HBO TV series *The Last of Us*, but the reality is just as spine-tingling.

The story begins when the fungus is just a spore, found on tropical forest floors. If the spore attaches to a passing ant, it makes its way through the insect's exoskeleton and begins to grow inside its body, whereby it's able to manipulate the ant's brain. The infected ant starts to behave strangely, in ways that support the survival and dispersal of the fungus—leaving its nest up in the canopy and spending more time down in the humid conditions of the forest floor. The end comes with the "death grip," which sees the ant climb up a plant then clamp its jaws onto the underside of a leaf, suspended above the ground at a height that enables an optimal dispersal of spores. Unable to release its grip, the ant dies in this position, as the fungus sends out hyphae to take over its body. Finally, a long stalk called a fruiting body, or "stroma," emerges from the host's head, to release new spores.

# Santa Claus and the magic reindeer

In the chilly regions of the Arctic, the indigenous Sámi peoples have herded reindeer for centuries. These reindeer love eating the *Amanita muscaria* mushroom, also known as the Fly Agaric or Fly Amanita (see page 54). Although poisonous for humans, when the mushroom is processed through a reindeer's kidneys (that is, when that reindeer's urine is drunk by a human), then it can be used as a powerful psychedelic drug. Among several theories, it's been proposed that this may have connections to the Christian imagery of Santa Claus and his reindeer.

During their mushroom-induced travels, Sámi shamans believed that they were able to turn into animals, fly as far as the North Star, then return to Earth and share their visions with the tribal elders, gathered in a yurt. Yurts have a firepit inside and a hole (chimney) at the top to allow the smoke to escape. With the shaman wearing red and white in honor of the mushroom itelf, it's not hard to see how this might have given rise to the concept of Santa Claus, flying with his herd of reindeer through the sky.

# What's the difference between mold and yeast?

Something you'll notice as you read on are references to molds and yeasts. Both belong to the Fungi kingdom, but it can be useful to know the difference between them. Molds are multicellular, growing in the form of hyphae (see page 11), and occurring in numerous colors. A common example of a mold is *Penicillium*. Yeasts, on the other hand, are colorless and consist of a single oval-shaped or spherical cell. A common example is *Candida*. As we'll see, molds are used in the production of foods and drugs, whereas yeasts are used to produce wine, beer, and bread.

# Twinkle twinkle . . . little earthstars

Earthstars may not taste good, and some species are poisonous, but they are certainly very beautiful. Imagine a ball in the center of a ray of stars, brown-gray in color. As the fungus ages, the rays turn back on themselves to reveal the round fruiting body. The spores then escape through a small hole called a "peristome." A typical earthstar measures some 4 inches (10 cm) across. They can be found in the leaf litter below beech trees or conifers, and even on grass verges. The Indigenous American Blackfoot people called them *ka-toos*, meaning "fallen stars," believing them to be indicators of supernatural events.

# Snow Fungus: skincare specialty

Also known as Silver Ear Fungus, White Cloud Ears, and White Jelly Mushroom, Snow Fungus (*Tremella fuciformis*) is often seen attached to fallen tree trunks or dead branches. Identified by its gelatinous white or translucent fronds, it's found mainly in tropical and subtropical regions, but is also seen in temperate regions in Asia, North America, and elsewhere.

Used in Chinese cooking to make sweet dishes, Snow Fungus has also been used for many years in Asian skincare products, and these are now becoming popular in the West. It is said to be gentle to the skin and beneficial in treating the effects of aging, boosting hydration and restoring elasticity.

# The truffle—an object of desire or just an expensive muddy lump?

The truffle—specifically the white truffle—is thought to be the world's rarest and most expensive ingredient, although of course there are several contenders jostling for prime position! The Alba, from northern Italy, weighs in at $330 per gram, for example, while the Matsutake—found in East and Southeast Asia, Eastern Europe, and the Pacific coast of North America—can cost $6,000 for a single specimen. But what exactly is a truffle, and why are they so prized?

Truffles are fungi—specifically, the sort of fungi that grow in a mycorrhizal relationship with trees, usually oaks. In appearance, they look a little like a potato, about the size of a golf ball. Since truffles attach to trees underground, we need to be able to find them. This task is often given to a specially trained dog or, more traditionally, a pig, both of which have a keen sense of smell. The need to train an animal for this task only adds to the expense of the fungus. And yet the truffle itself, while a holy grail for those who find its pheromone-like scent extraordinarily desirable, is almost repugnant to others.

# Colorful mushrooms

Did you know that some mushrooms can be used to make natural dyes for fabrics? There are a few mushrooms that are even named for this, including the Dyer's Puffball (*Pisolithus arhizus*) and the Dyer's Polypore (*Phaeolus arhizus*).

A number of different fungi can be used, providing a vast array of interesting shades. The Golden Chanterelle, for example, produces oranges and yellows, while many of the red-capped fungi (including *Russulas*) produce shades of red or brown, and *Lactarius indigo* (Indigo Milkcap) results in a deep purple or indigo. But for the results to last there needs to be a matching "mordant" that fixes the color. For example, the King Bolete has a mordant of ammonia, giving a red-yellow hue, as does the Meadow Mushroom (resulting in yellow-green).

# Yeast extract

If you love the delicious umami flavor of yeast extract, perhaps for breakfast on toast, then you might be surprised to learn that the production of this popular thick, dark spread depends on ... beer! The main ingredient is a concentrated extract of brewer's yeast, which in turn is a byproduct of the beer-brewing industry, created during fermentation. Yeast extract doesn't actually contain any alcohol at all, although it does contain B vitamins, which provide a range of health benefits, including skin generation and blood circulation.

# Mycoproteins—fungi for saving the planet

Although you might have eaten Quorn, you might not have realized that it's made from fungus. Launched in 1985, the backstory of this meat substitute reads like a science-fiction movie! Scientists at the time were worried that population growth and greenhouse gas emissions might leave the planet unable to support a global famine, so, just like in the movies, they set out to save us. The hero was a fungus, *Fusarium venenatum*, discovered growing in a soil sample in the U.K.

The fungus is still grown commercially (and of course there are now many other brands offering their own mycroprotein products). And the name? It was inspired by the Quorn Hunt, going strong since 1696. It's quite ironic that one of the world's oldest fox hunts provided the name for a meat-free food alternative!

# Witches' Butter

If you happen to spot a particular wobbly yellow "thing" seemingly stuck to dead wood, you may not realize that it's a fungus at all. This is *Tremella mesenterica*, aka the Yellow Brain Fungus, or Witches' Butter. Found in deciduous and mixed forests in North and South America, Eurasia, and Australia, there's some interesting folklore behind this odd specimen. According to one belief, if Witches' Butter appeared stuck to the gate of a house, it signified that a witch had cast a spell on its inhabitants. The only way to counteract this was to stick pins in the fungus!

To confuse matters, there's also another fungus that goes by the name of Witches' Butter—*Exidia glandulosa*, found on dead wood and widely distributed throughout the northern hemisphere. This black, squidgy, gelatinous species is very witchy-looking indeed, even more so than its yellow counterpart.

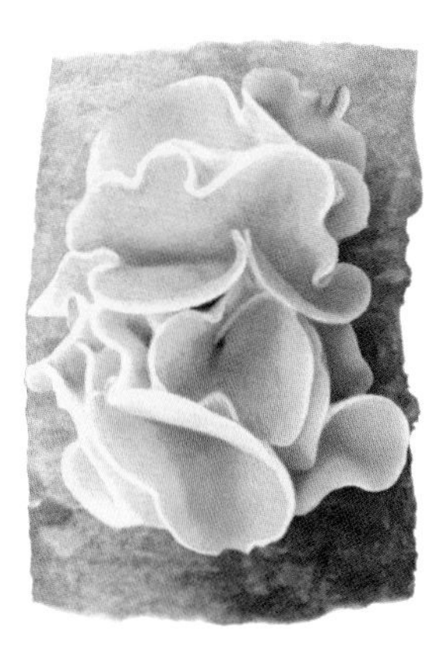

# Earth-friendly produce

Mushrooms happen to be one of the world's most sustainably produced food sources. Here are some quick facts:

- Mushrooms need only limited space to grow. Just 1 acre (0.4 hectares) can produce up to a million pounds (450,000 kg) of mushrooms each year.
- Mushrooms require very little energy to grow—they grow in the dark and only require a small amount of electricity to harvest.
- Mushrooms require very little water compared to fruit and vegetables—less than 2 gallons (7.5 liters) of water are needed to produce 1 pound (0.5 kg) of button mushrooms.

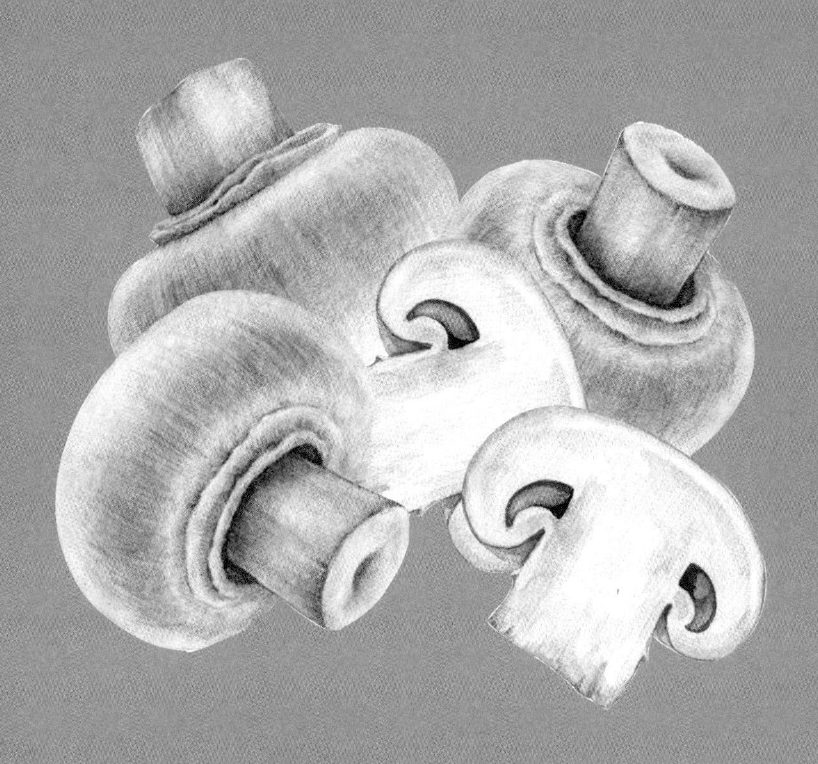

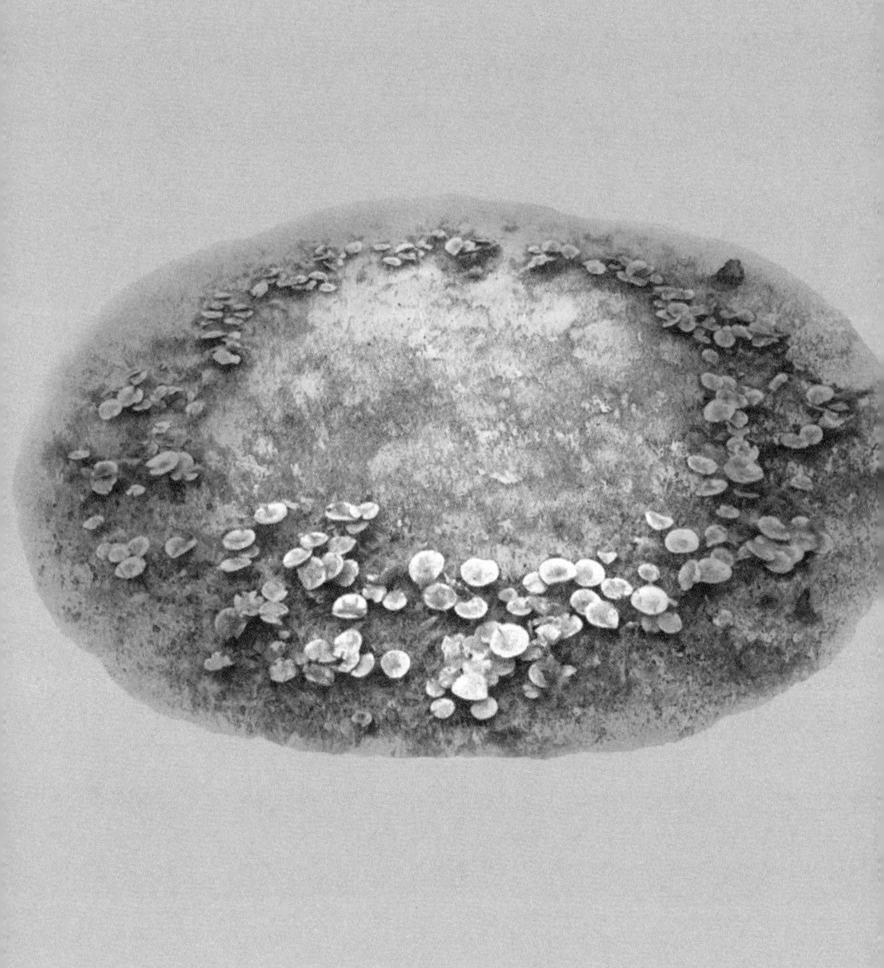

# Fairy Rings

Fairy Rings, or Fairy Circles, are naturally occurring round patches of mushrooms that appear in woodlands and grasslands and can occur year after year. Cultures all around the world have been entranced by the apparent magic of fairy rings, making them the subject of countless myths and folklore. What *is* known about fairy rings is that once a spore finds a suitable location for growing, they germinate and then grow outward from the middle. This creates a ring shape, with mushrooms appearing around the edges of the circle. Several types of mushrooms can create fairy rings. European folklore enchants with tales of these magical rings as the chosen place where fairies frolic. However, fairy rings can be dangerous for mere mortals. One step into a fairy ring, and the unsuspecting human may be transported to the fairy realm, unable to escape the fairies' powerful spell.

# Mushroom tinctures and powders

Mushroom tinctures are purported to offer a wide range of health benefits, including immune system and mental health support, skin health in the form of anti-aging and wound-healing, and enhancement of athletic performance. Tinctures are liquid extracts made by soaking mushrooms in alcohol and water. While many healers and practitioners around the world have validated these benefits for centuries, scientific studies are ongoing to steadfastly support these claims.

Common mushrooms used in tinctures include Chaga, Lion's Mane, Reishi, Cordyceps, Turkey Tail, Shiitake, Maitake, and more. The Turkey Tail mushroom is believed to have potential cancer-fighting properties. The Chaga mushroom has anti-inflammatory properties and can be useful in preventing chronic disease. Lion's Mane mushroom is believed to aid anxiety, depression, and brain function. Cordyceps is believed to boost energy. Enoki mushrooms are thought to boost immunity for their anti-viral and anti-inflammatory properties. Mushroom tinctures can be store-bought or made at home, as long as extreme caution is adhered to. Mushroom tinctures are meant to be ingested orally. Some people add these tinctures to drinks or foods, such as coffee or soup, while others drop them directly under their tongue. Mushroom powders are dried mushrooms also taken medicinally for health-boosting effects. They have similar results but are produced differently. In this case, mushrooms are dehydrated rather than soaked in liquid. Some people sprinkle this powder on top of food, but many find that the powder needs to be heated to improve flavor and aroma.

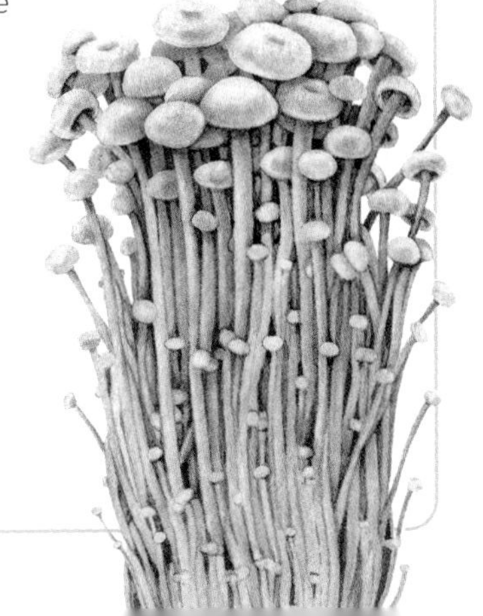

# Mushroom picking: 10 top tips

*It's worth knowing from the start that fungi don't always do as they're told—in other words, even though there are some tried and true "rules" for finding them, and even if conditions are perfect, they don't always reveal themselves. The good news, though, is that you don't need lots of equipment (unless, of course, you want it). Our recommendations are to take a basket or canvas bag, a knife, and some gloves.*

1. The best times for finding mushrooms are mid-spring and mid-fall. But don't let that stop you from looking at other times.

2. Be patient. Mushrooms can pop up in the same places, year on year, but also in places that you'd never expect. The sacks from commercial garden compost will sometimes offer a nice surprise.

3. Mushrooms often appear two or three weeks after a good drenching, so put the date in your diary.

4. Get to know your trees. Seek out areas that have a mix of deciduous trees and conifers.

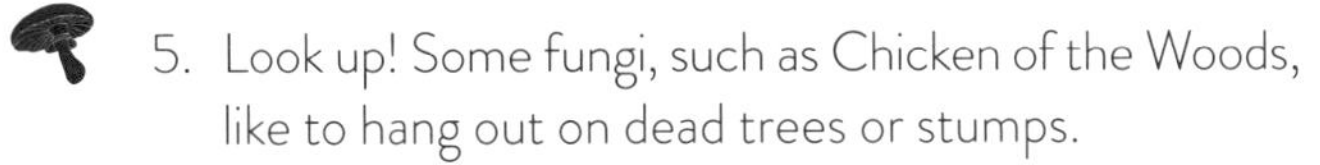

5. Look up! Some fungi, such as Chicken of the Woods, like to hang out on dead trees or stumps.

6. Look down! Others can be found clinging to fallen branches, such as Scarlet Elf Caps.

7. Go to the library or a bookstore and buy some good mushrooming books.

8. The sight of Fly Agaric, especially near beech trees, is often an indication that there are other mushrooms in the area.

9. Don't be disappointed if you can't find anything. Tomorrow is another day.

10. Finally, don't think it's just about edibility. Even a thwarted foraging expedition will leave you feeling happy.

MUSHROOM
RECIPES

The mushrooms in these recipes are interchangeable, meaning that if you can't find the specific mushroom suggested, you can replace it with a safe, edible alternative. Most importantly, though, please exercise caution when consuming wild and foraged mushrooms. This book recommends using mushrooms from a farm store or market that have been clearly assessed for safety; however, if you choose to ingest wild mushrooms, be sure to carefully identify and thoroughly wash and prepare them, and consume them at your own risk.

If you do pick your own mushrooms, always make sure they're fresh, with a good scent. It's also a good idea not to pick too many because wild mushrooms generally don't have much of a shelf life. It's also worth remembering that if you go on a foraging expedition but it turns out to be fruitless—or you just prefer the reassurance of mushrooms identified by an expert—high-quality, store-bought ingredients mean you'll always be able to treat yourself to one of these delicious dishes!

# Cauliflower Mushroom Cheese

*Serves 4–6*

Since Cauliflower Mushrooms are so similar in appearance to cauliflowers, it seems right and proper to celebrate the resemblance by using them to make a variation of cauliflower cheese.

## Ingredients

1 fresh Cauliflower Mushroom, around 8 inches (20 cm) wide, thoroughly cleaned and free of mud, insects, and leaves

3½ tbsp (50 g) butter or a vegan substitute

⅓ cup (50 g) all-purpose (plain) flour

1 quart (1 liter) whole (full-fat) milk or vegan alternative (oat milk works well)

6 oz (160 g) Cheddar cheese or vegan alternative

Handful of breadcrumbs (optional)

Salt and freshly ground pepper

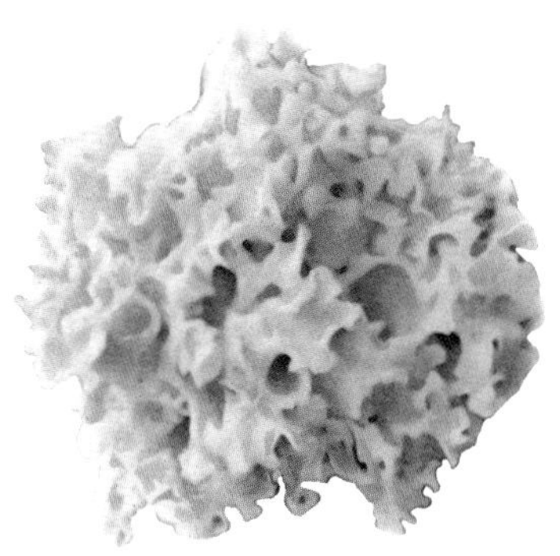

## Method

1. Preheat the oven to 350°F/180°C/Gas Mark 4.
2. Using a sharp knife, cut the mushroom into chunks roughly measuring 2 inches (5 cm) across. Place them in a baking dish and leave to one side.
3. Melt the butter or vegan alternative in large, heavy saucepan over a low heat.
4. Gently stir in the flour and cook for 2 minutes, taking care not to let the mixture (the roux) stick to the pan.
5. Remove the pan from the heat and add the milk or vegan substitute to the roux a little at a time, stirring continuously, to make a sauce.
6. Put the pan back on the heat and stir it steadily, bringing the sauce to a gentle boil.
7. Stir in the cheese of choice and let it melt. Add salt and pepper to taste.
8. Pour the cheese sauce over the mushroom chunks, scatter the breadcrumbs (if using) over the top, then bake for 40 minutes until golden and bubbling.
9. Let the dish cool a little, then serve it with some crusty bread.

# Chicken of the Woods in Breadcrumbs

*Serves 4*

Both the color and the texture of this mushroom are SO very much like chicken that this may not be a favorite for vegans and vegetarians. However, this recipe is a great example of just how close fungi can be to meat in terms of flavor, texture, and appearance.

## Ingredients

Chicken of the Woods, allowing about 8 "nuggets"—or slices, around 6 x 4 inches (15 x 10 cm)—per person

2 cups (130 g) fresh breadcrumbs

Pinch of paprika or garlic powder

3 eggs (or a vegan substitute)

4 tbsp vegetable oil

3½ tbsp (50 g) butter or a vegan substitute

Salt and freshly ground pepper

## Method

1. Thoroughly wash the mushrooms and pat them dry, disposing of any of the tough parts that might have might have been attached to the tree that the mushrooms were found growing on.
2. Put the breadcrumbs, salt and pepper, and paprika or garlic powder into a bowl.
3. Beat the eggs in a separate bowl.
4. Dip the mushroom pieces in the egg, then toss them in the breadcrumb mix, coating each piece thoroughly.
5. Add the oil and butter or vegan substitute to a pan or wok. (Adding oil to the butter will prevent it from burning.) When hot, add the mushroom pieces, tossing them regularly so that they don't catch in the pan.
6. Shake the cooked mushroom pieces out onto paper towel or a clean towel to absorb excess oil, then serve them with a salad, potato wedges, and tomato ketchup.

# Giant Puffball Steaks

*Serves 4–6*

If you're wanting to cook something using a Giant Puffball, this is about the easiest recipe there is—the ingredients could not be simpler or more delicious, and it will appeal to carnivores, vegans, and vegetarians. You'll notice that cutting the puffball with a bread knife, which has a serrated edge, creates little grooves in the flesh, making the slices look more meaty and steak-like!

## Ingredients

1 fresh Giant Puffball, cleaned of soil or grass

1 knob of butter or a vegan substitute

1 tbsp oil

Crushed garlic, 1–2 cloves (or more, depending on preference)

Soy sauce, to taste

### Method

1. Using a bread knife, cut the Puffball into slices roughly 2 inches (5 cm) thick.
2. Heat the butter or vegan substitute and oil in a pan over a medium heat, then add the garlic with a generous glug of soy sauce. As the garlic starts to sizzle, add the Puffball slices. As they cook, turn each of the slices carefully with a spatula so that they all get covered in plenty of soy sauce and garlic. As the individual slices cook, you might find it easier to remove them from the pan and pop them into a warm oven to stay nice and hot until the rest of the steaks are done.
3. Add a wild greens side salad and buttery mashed potatoes, then enjoy!

# Morels on Toast

*Serves 6*

Chefs prize the Morel for its flavor—so much so that the way of cooking them is usually kept as simple as possible. This distinctive earthy flavor, combined with an interesting spongy texture, is why these mushrooms are often described as being toasty, meaty, or a bit like bread. To honor this king among fungi, it seems only right to follow in the footsteps of those French chefs who revere it. Do what they do and simply sauté the mushrooms in plenty of butter, season well, then pile them onto warm, crusty bread.

## Ingredients

At least 2 tbsp olive oil

Generous knob of butter or a vegan substitute

36 fresh Morels (6 per person), cleaned thoroughly and dried using paper towel or a clean towel

6 slices of crusty bread (preferably sourdough)

Sea salt and freshly ground pepper

### Method

1. Slowly heat the oil and butter in a heavy-bottomed pan, and once they are hot enough, add the Morels.
2. Stir the Morels gently until they become fragrant.
3. Place the slices of bread on separate plates, then distribute the contents of the pan evenly between them, finishing off with salt and pepper to taste.

**DISCLAIMER:**

Morels contain a toxin—possibly hydrazine—that can cause gastrointestinal illness, sometimes with fatal consequences. So be sure to always cook them before consuming; the cooking process removes the toxin.

# Sautéed Scarlet Elf Cups

*Serves 4*

This dish is a real seasonal treat. Found hidden in woodland areas any time from late winter to early spring, Scarlet Elf Cups can be found attached to branches and also on the ground. This is a small fungus, measuring up to around 2¼ inches (6 cm) in diameter, but being bright red, it's easy to spot. Turn it over and, although not always visible, you might see an orange stem underneath.

## Ingredients

1 knob of butter or a vegan substitute

1 tbsp olive oil

Crushed garlic, 1–2 cloves (or more if you wish)

40 Scarlet Elf Cups (10 per person), washed, cleaned, and patted dry

Squeeze of lemon juice

Salt and freshly ground pepper

### Method

1. Add the butter or vegan substitute and oil to a heavy pan and heat them over a low heat. Add the crushed garlic and shake the pan to cook it evenly.
2. After 2 or 3 minutes, add the Elf Cups. They won't take long to cook; 5 to 8 minutes will be plenty. Season them to taste with the lemon juice and salt and pepper, then use them however you prefer—served on crusty bread, chopped and used in savory pancakes, or even added to kedgeree!

# Forager's Breakfast

*Serves 4*

The ultimate forager's breakfast, wild mushrooms on toast is an excellent way to appreciate your foraged treasures in a hearty meal—or to enjoy a delicious haul from your local farmers' market. Add fresh herbs, sliced ham or prosciutto, or crème fraiche for extra indulgence—or keep things simple (and vegan!) with the recipe opposite.

## Ingredients

12 oz (350 g) mixed wild mushrooms

4 large slices sourdough bread

1 tbsp olive oil

Butter or vegan substitute, plus extra for frying (optional)

1 garlic clove, crushed

Handful of fresh herbs, such as parsley or thyme (optional)

## Method

1. Wash and prepare your mushrooms. If using larger mushrooms or a mix of mushrooms, slice to ensure all are of a similar size. This will ensure even cooking.
2. Toast the sourdough bread, butter lightly, then set aside. Place 1 slice on each plate.
3. Heat a large frying pan with olive oil or butter, as desired. Add the mushrooms and cook for 2 minutes, followed by the garlic. Cook for 3–4 more minutes.
4. Top the prepared toasts with the garlic mushrooms and sprinkle with fresh herbs. Enjoy!

# Homemade Truffle Oil

*Makes ½ cup (120 ml)*

This simple recipe is ideal for adding a little truffle extravagance to jazz up any meal. Truffles have an incredibly rich, umami flavor and strong aroma. With a limited growing season, delicious truffles are only available for a short period. Truffle oil can be made with white truffles (usually from Italy) and black truffles (usually from France), with subtle flavor differences between the two. White has a subtler, more mushroom-like flavor. Black has a stronger, more earthy flavor.

Note—truffle oil is best used as a finishing oil. This means that it is best suited to drizzling over a meal once it has been prepared. Truffle oil is not to be used for cooking, and the flavor reduces when introduced to high heat. Truffle oil is best used in moderation. Remember, use in small amounts—you can always add more!

## Ingredients

1–2 tbsp truffles, shaved

½ cup (120 ml) neutrally flavored oil, such as olive oil or grapeseed oil

## Method

1. Shave/finely grate your truffle using a mandoline or microplane and measure out 1–2 tablespoons.
2. Over a low heat, warm the oil in a saucepan on the stove. It is important to ensure the temperature does not exceed 130°F/55°C, as higher heat can affect truffles' flavor.
3. Remove the saucepan from the stove and add 1–2 tablespoons of shaved truffles to the oil. Leave the truffles to steep in the oil as it cools down to room temperature.
4. Truffle oil will last for up to 3 days refrigerated. For best results, use it immediately. Sprinkle over pastas and risottos for an instant gourmet meal at home.

# INDEX

# ACKNOWLEDGEMENTS AND CREDITS

This book is dedicated to Henry Ashby, submariner and forager, no longer with us but remembered fondly by the foraging fraternity that loved him, and to our incredible friend and designer, Jacqui Caulton.

Cover illustrations: AnitaPol, courtesy of Shutterstock

Interior illustrations:
AnitaPol (courtesty of Shutterstock): pages 4, 5, 6-7, 8, 9, 11, 12, 13, 14, 15, 16, 18 (top and right), 19, 20-21, 27, 28, 31, 36, 40, 47, 51, 52, 55, 56, 59, 60, 63, 68, 71, 72, 75, 76, 79, 80, 83, 84, 86-87, 88, 89, 92, 96, 100, 101, 105, 107, 108, 109, 110 (left and right), 115, 119, 120, 121, 122-123, 124, 125, 128, 130, 132, 134, 136, 139.

Lisa Alderson: pages 10, 18 (left), 23, 24, 32, 35, 39, 43, 44, 48, 64, 67, 91, 95, 98, 102, 110 (center), 113, 116, 118, 126.

The recipes on pages 126-135 are reproduced with permission from *Foraging with Kids* © Adele Nozedar/Watkins Publishing.

# ADDITIONAL RESOURCES

**Books**

*Fungi of Temperate Europe*, vols. 1 and 2, by Thomas Laesso and Jens H. Petersen, Princeton University (2019)

*Collins Complete British Mushrooms & Toadstools* by Paul Sterry and Barry Hughes, Collins (2009)

*Mushrooms and other fungi of Great Britain and Europe* by Roger Phillips, Macmillan (2006)—This book is a classic, well worth space on your shelf. Phillips wrote several nature-based books and is no longer with us, but his legacy is curated by his daughter and his books are very much alive. Find him on Instagram at @Rogerphillips_redglasses

*Entangled Life* by Merlin Sheldrake, Vintage (2021)

*Finding the Mother Tree* by Suzanne Simard, Allen Lane (2022)

*How To Change Your Mind: The New Science of Psychedelics* by Michael Pollan, Penguin (2019—also a film of the same name)—Pollan discovers first-hand how LSD and psilocybin can be used in unlikely, but moving and incredible ways.

*Wild Food UK Mushroom Guide* by Marlow Renton, Otherwise (2023)

*Growing Gourmet and Medicinal Mushrooms* by Paul Stamets, Ten Speed Press (2011)

*Mycelium Running: How Mushrooms Can Help Save The World* by Paul Stamets, Ten Speed Press (2005)

#### Mushroom Organizations

The Mycological Society of America: www.msafungi.org

The North American Mycological Association: www.namyco.org

The British Mycological Society: www.britmycolsoc.org.uk

The Association of Foragers: www.foragers-association.org

The Fungus Conservation Trust: www.fungustrust.org.uk

#### Podcasts

"No Fungi, No Future" on Spotify
—exploring the impact that fungi have on our lives

"The Magic of Mushrooms" on BBC Sounds
—The Infinite Monkey Cage with Professor Brian Cox and Robin Ince, featuring Merlin Sheldrake, author of *Entangled Life*

"The Mushroom Network" on Apple
—the space where fungi meets science

#### Apps and Websites

"Shroomify" mushroom ID app for the U.S.A. and U.K.

www.first-nature.com—A fantastic resource, impeccably researched and easy to search for. All proceeds go toward conservation work.

www.gallowaywildfoods.com—There are many brilliant foragers on the planet, including Mark Williams of Galloway Wild Foods, whose site is clear, comprehensive, and full of character.

#### Films

*The Last of Us*—A video game before it became a horror movie, it was inspired by the shuddersome habit of the Cordyceps fungus, which, in the film, evolves to survive in human bodies.

*Fantastic Fungi*—This is a must-watch documentary, beautifully filmed and full of hope for our future.

# ABOUT THE AUTHOR

Adele Nozedar is a forager, author, and foraging guide. She has been featured in *National Geographic*, the *New York Times*, and in countless other U.K. and U.S.A. magazines and newspapers.
Her foraging titles include (with Penguin/Square Peg) *The Hedgerow Handbook* and *The Garden Forager* and (with Watkins) *The Tree Forager* and *Foraging with Kids*. She is proud to have been amongst the group of that founded the Foragers' Association (www.foragers-association.org). Her favorite mushroom is the *Boletus edulis*.